HUMAN ASSETS

"Unleash Your People, Propel Your Company"

Daniel J. Shrader

Copyright, 2106 by Daniel J. Shrader

For information on this book or conference and seminar information contact the author at
www.danjshrader@gmail.com

All rights reserved. No part of this book may be used or reproduced in any manner whatsoever without the written permission of the author.

Coming December 2016, "Power, Take It."

By Daniel J. Shrader

Copyright, 2016 by Daniel J. Shrader

CONTENTS

Are You in Trouble	1
Zombie Employees	8
Leadership and Middle Management	12
Leadership	21
Unleash Your Human Assets	33
Getting Started	
Mind Set	55
Perfection	63
What Failure Looks Like	68
Trust, Respect and Admiration	75
When is the Passion Gone?	82

Every Day Exceptional Leaders	87
George Murray	88
Sam Taylor	91
Bill Titler	94
Conclusion	98
About the Author	102

TO MY FRIENDS AND COLLEAGUES,

NEVER GIVE UP, NEVER QUIT

ALWAYS STRIVE FOR SUCCESS

FORWARD

This work is the result of my interactions with hundreds of companies and organizations on all levels over the last four decades. What I continually ran into was that virtually all of these companies had reached some level of success but had never reached the point of breaking out to becoming the best in their industry. Though they had similar products and services to their competitors, they were not number one in their industry. They were just part of the crowd of players. It was a common frustration as though there was some invisible ceiling that kept them from becoming the best.

The number one players always had one thing in common which was innovation that was unique to them alone. They were always one step if not several steps ahead of their competition in innovation on all levels. Not just the best products and services but also the best way to make these products, the best way to market and sell these products, the best way to purchase their supplies, and more, basically they are better in every area. They are the most efficient and the best at what they do. The rest of the industry is always playing catch up by spending the bulk of their time and energy learning what the number one player is doing and trying to copy them when possible.

It's so obvious that the distinct ingredient to always being the number one player is continual innovation. I had to ask myself why they always win on innovation and the others don't.

The answer turned out to be very simple. It was the environment that their employees worked in versus the environment at the other players. It was an environment of leadership throughout the entire organization that led to deep employee engagement that then led to high performance and continual innovation. These companies always had very low turnover. They had discovered the key ingredient that led to the employees being very loyal, highly energized and highly engaged in the success of the company. It turns out these employees love their companies and as such are hard to dislodge from their employer.

What I found to be the most interesting was that any company can do this if they simply know how to do it and if they decide to do it.

This is the result of interaction with hundreds of companies from small startups that excelled to large Fortune 500 companies that no one could catch. I personally have used these techniques in companies that I have run and it worked every time.

Perhaps like many of you, I have read many books and attended numerous seminars on this subject. They were inspirational and motivating at the same time but there always seemed to be something missing. My observation was that the words they all used were similar if not the same. After the excitement was over, I realized that they never actually told you how to do it in specific detail.

Unlike so many other books, periodicals and seminars on the subject I wanted to give you the exact steps you can apply to make this happen. I've even given you the exact words to use and when, that will trigger an environment that will lead to high employee engagement, innovation and superior performance. The examples contained herein are numerous and all involve real companies and real people. What is not here is continual theory and quotes by people who have never actually run a company or led a group of people to achieve greatness. What is also not here are endless charts and diagrams that are really just meant to fill empty pages. The impossible is possible when the employees "want" to do it. I will give you the keys as to how you can make this happen.

I hope that you enjoy this and that you can also make this work for your organization.

Are You in Trouble

Yes, You Are in Trouble.

It's the middle of the night, your phone rings and the caller on the other line says your building is on fire or your production line equipment is being damaged or your inventory is being stolen out the back door.

What do you do?

Perhaps it goes like this. You hop in your car, race to your business, making calls along the way to bring together as many people and resources as you can to mitigate the damage and put an end to the losses.

Or maybe.

It's the middle of the work day, your phone rings and it's a key manager who says, they just found out your key technology is being copied by a competitor or that your patents are being willfully violated or that a competitor has just taken your largest clients away or that a competitor has just introduced a new product or service at a reduced price that makes yours uncompetitive if not even obsolete.

What do you do?

Perhaps it goes like this. You cancel the rest of your day and bring together all key senior management in an emergency meeting. Your assets are being impaired, you're losing your best customers. You're now in trouble.

We'll come back to this in a minute.

We measure and account for our key assets in various financial reports such as profit and loss statements, balance sheets, etc. to name a few. They account for our patents, equipment, inventory, vehicles, furniture, and more. After all, these are the key assets that allow us to operate and succeed. The tools of our business, the products we sell, and the services we provide. Of course we need to protect them at all costs. We hold endless meetings to that end.

You might know where I'm going with this but let's continue on.

As to the two scenarios laid out above the actions taken have one thing in common. It's that you stop all other activity and take action.

So what's missing?

In all of the various financial statements that value your business the one thing missing are the employees. Not in a single financial statement or list of your assets is there any accounting for or value assigned to your employees.

Think about this.

New products or services don't just invent themselves. The competitive edge to those products or services did not just happen on its own. How we market, sell and price those products in a way that excels beyond any competitor isn't just a matter of luck. This list goes on and on, how we manufacture, how we purchase on time, how we inventory, etc.

All of these things happen because of people. The better and more committed the people the better these things happen.

All innovation comes from people. So remember this one thing. The very moment a company stops innovating it starts dying. Your current competitors and I would say even the future competitors you don't even know about yet are dedicated to one thing. They are dedicated to taking your customers by beating you on every level.

The one asset, your most important asset, which can keep your competitors from your throat, your employees, are unhappy, unmotivated, disengaged and looking to leave you. Every employee study indicates the majority of all employees on all levels are unhappy and unfulfilled with their current job.

So if your response is something like the following. We pay very competitive wages and benefits and we have a very robust talent acquisition team that is constantly seeking out the best talent. Additionally, we utilize state of the art software to filter candidates and then further utilize sophisticated psychological testing to determine the strengths of our candidates and employees who work at our company. And finally, we have a committee made up senior members of our Human Resource Department that work on creating a positive work environment. Well, you're in trouble.

Unlike the extensive actions taken to protect the assets in the first two scenarios, most organizations give very little attention to protecting their Human Assets. The proof of this is simple, most employees are unhappy in their jobs.

We'll talk about what creates this situation and what needs to happen to change this for both the benefit of the company and the employees. Employees used to just grab a job if it was offered but in today's world their being more selective. You need to understand that there are best of breed people who will never work at your company for various reasons. This can be changed though. Worse than not attracting the best people is that your best current employees are looking for other employment as you read these words. If you don't believe this, then you're not in trouble you're in big trouble.

When I meet with the owners of a business or an officer or departmental manager of a business I always ask this question in a very specific way. I ask, "On a personal level what is your number one frustration with your employees as it relates to your business and you?" The answers are virtually always the same. They say that no one seems to be doing anything or no one gets anything done and out frustration they'll say they are tired of having to personally do everything. Their feelings are honest and in many cases right. They are having to push every ball forward every day as if no one else seemed to care.

What we're going to cover is why it is this way and how do you create an environment wherein everything his hitting on every cylinder and on every level.

The key is to create a leadership environment that causes the employees to fully engage the business with the result being performance and innovation thru ought the entire organization. We'll provide you with real life examples that you can use to get this to happen. The word engagement is commonly used in the business world but no one actually shows you how to make it happen. They don't tell you what has to happen first, the ground work that needs to be established, between the manager and the employee. Further, once the ground work has been established they don't tell you exactly how to trigger the events that will result in the full employee engagement. We'll do that.

If you do this you won't have a feeling of having to do everything yourself, instead you'll spend your time marveling in the success of your business or organization.

Remember this as you continue reading. Great leaders and great organizations don't just happen. Leadership development is deep in the DNA of these organizations and both the employee and organization benefit together.

After starting this you will see great results that are transformative and going forward from there you will become very deliberate in making sure that this new environment of leadership development is never side tracked, never allowed to stop.

The following will be repeated a number of times in the book because it's one of the keys to making this effort successful for you. "They will hear your words but will judge you on your actions." Never forget these words, they are one of the keys you'll need to cause full engagement and the unleashing of your people.

In the next couple of chapters I'm going to lay some ground work as to the current environment that exists in most organizations. It's important to know where you are so that you can get perspective as to where you need to go.

Zombie Employees

Your employees have stopped caring. You say it cannot be true. They show up on time every day. The ones you pass in the hallways say good morning. Their reports are on time, they attend all meetings and have pictures on their desks.

Zombie employees are those that show up on time and go thru their daily duties but they have stopped caring. The result is they do only what's necessary to keep their jobs. Most of them are looking for a new job or at a minimum are open to leaving if the right opportunity were offered. They tell their family and friends that their unhappy in their job and with the company they work for. They spend evenings and weekends on the various job sites looking to see what's available.

Two things are happening here. One is they have disengaged emotionally from the company they're at, your company, and secondly in sharing their feeling with family and friends they are spreading the word that your company is not a place where one should want to work. This absolutely can affect future recruiting.

Earlier we posed the question of what would you do if your inventory was going out the back door, stolen, or your equipment was being damaged in such a way that it was no longer operating in a productive way. Remember, your employees are your most valuable asset. They are preparing to pour out the door or just as bad if not worse, like the damaged equipment, they are no longer as productive as they could be. They have stopped working in a way that could propel your company to the next level. These are your zombie employees. They don't want to be like this. The environment that their company has allowed to exist has made them this way. Their drive and creativity are now gone.

If you care about your company you have to care about this. If you knew the true percentage of your employees that feel this way you would be sickened.

We all know that most businesses fail. It's not just the start ups. Ask yourself how many old line multi-billion dollar revenue companies ended up in the corporate cemetery. At what point did these companies stop innovating and start dying. We know all innovation comes from people so at what point did the employees stop caring, and as such just start showing up each day but no longer innovating.

This is not the employees fault. Its managements fault. Now with that said, most CEO's and founders of companies have unquestioned drive and passion for their company. Their ideas and inspiration are endless much like an evangelist on a mission.

The failure is in the next layers of management that filter down thru the organizational chart. Not all of them but certainly many if not most of them. We'll talk about what's going wrong and the solutions later.

Don't waste your time trying to figure out who the zombie employees are so that you can replace them. It's not the solution or where you need to focus your attention.

To make you think about this I want you to do an exercise right now if you would. I want you to read no further until you first take out a piece of paper and a pen and do the following. I want you to write down the names of the various managers in your organization that you know without a doubt whose employees would walk thru fire for them. I want you to be careful that it's not the managers you like or that you think some of the employees might like but the ones who have commanded such a level of respect, trust and admiration that the employees would do the impossible for them.

If you're being honest with yourself the list is not very long is it.

Now I want you to do one last exercise. I want you, before you read any further, to leave your office right now and walk thru your business for 20 minutes. I want you to look at the people you pass and beyond the courtesy hello you'll here I want you to think about each employee. I want you to ask yourself if you truly believe they are fully engaged in the success of the business, along with the innovation and improvements that can take the business to the next level. Do they care about their superiors, or even care about you for that fact? I want you to think about whether the honest answer is, that they really are only doing what's required to keep their jobs and get the paycheck.

We'll talk in more detail later about this in, "When the Passion is Gone".

Leadership and Middle Management

Let's start by saying what leadership is not. True leaders are not born from a title. This is the first big mistake. Many of you have heard of the Peter Principal, which I have seen over and over again in many of the organizations I have touched. It goes basically like this. Employees as they do well are continually promoted to more responsible positions with a greater number of employees and sub-managers answering to them until they are no longer effective in their management position. This once rising star, who is now over their head, is now hurting the organization on a number of levels. History shows they then stay at that management position affecting all that answer to them because they are no longer affective. Not only are the employees who answer up to them and seek their leadership unhappy, they themselves are unhappy. Rarely are these managers removed or reassigned.

To protect their position, this ineffective manager tends to hold back those under them. The ineffective manager knows that they are not going to move higher in the organization so to nurture, lead, develop and promote those under them would only make them eventually obsolete.

Management that uses threats, whether stated or subtle, to push their employees is not leadership. This only creates zombie employees. When employees say they hate their job their saying they hate and don't respect their manager. If you want to destroy employee drive, creativity and moral allow their manager to threaten them. I actually consulted with a company where one of the managers believed that the way you got employees to respect you was to get them to fear you. The moral was horrible and the turnover was 50% per year. This type of manager is so prevalent in corporate America you would be shocked. They exist everywhere and yet they are relatively invisible to the management above them. The threats are usually subtle in nature and I would tell you that they are so far from true leadership that you simply need to get rid of them before they completely destroy your employee base. I would further add, that if you're employee working for a manager of this type and the company doesn't do anything about it than free yourself by turning in your resignation. Don't worry, these employees aren't going to quit because I tell them to, they're going to quit because they want to. We're going to talk about employees doing something because they "want to" later.

Managers who don't hit a goal and then blame their team or a specific team member are not leaders. Leaders take responsibility.

Managers who have high turnover in their employees are not leaders, their failures. High employee turnover is one of the number one signs of failed leadership.

Managers who avoid tough decisions are not leaders, they're weak.

Managers who hold back star employees for fear that the employee will outshine the manager are not leaders. This is also very common in many of the organizations I have advised. Its fear on the manager's part of not looking valuable to their superiors. This type of manager is very insecure. The star employees will leave once they realize their future is capped because of this manager.

Who has ever heard the phrase, "Company Politics"? It's derogatory and refers to all of the games that are necessary for the employee to survive and succeed within a dysfunctional organization. Company politics can be laid directly at the feet of your managers. It's an environment created by and allowed to proliferate by your bad managers. It is one of the signs of bad management and shows a complete lack of understanding of leadership development within the organization.

I have been involved with companies on one level or another for 36 years and during that entire time I have continually heard from management that, "we have the word leadership in the employees job description, so what's the problem". To simply say or write the word leadership does not make it happen. The ability to lead is more important than any other quality or skill an employee or manager can have. Just as your people are not quantified in your organizations assets the leadership qualities they possess are given at best a courtesy level of attention.

The goal is to encourage leadership, employee engagement and innovation. The innovation will come from employee engagement which is a result of great leadership. There are many steps to each process and each step moves smoothly unless there are roadblocks that cannot be overcome. Now, there are no natural roadblocks that cannot be overcome only the one's put in place by ineffective management. These are like big red stop signs to the process that are in virtually all cases put in place by management. Leadership should be explaining on a continual basis that the company's success is born from innovation and without innovation the company fails and as such the employees all fail. Most importantly, it being encouraged and required that all employees participate in the innovation of the company. The path to innovation is accomplishing high employee engagement which is only possible when the employees want to do what they do versus having to do it to keep their jobs. Engagement is the result of leadership development on all employee levels, which requires great managers who understand this and act on developing it daily.

Let me explain the following situation. This situation occurs somewhere within virtually every company that has ever existed. It goes like this. An employee has an idea that is maybe great or maybe not. Most ideas really aren't that great but that's not the point here. So the employee goes to his or her manager and says, hey boss I've got an idea for the _____. Here comes the stop sign in the response from the manager, "Not now maybe later" or "Our plans are already in place" or "Send me an email" or finally the worst response assuming the manager bothered to even here the idea, "I'll get back to you". This response really means, I'll never get back to you and I don't value either you or your ideas. The employee will attempt a few more times to approach the manager on the idea but will continually here, "I'll get back to you". This is the stop sign to leadership development, engagement and innovation. Everyone reading these words has seen this happen over and over again. Perhaps you have done this yourself.

The manager here is doing this for various reasons. The big one could be they are simply incapable of making a decision so they put everything off. By saying, "I'll get back to you", over and over again is really a way to get the employee to give up and go away. Trust me, they will give up and they will go away by leaving and going to another employer. This manager is putting up big stop signs to innovation and at the same time completely destroying the worth of the employee. Word of this behavior on the manager's part absolutely spreads thru the organization and says that your ideas really are not wanted, so stop trying. The other thing happening here is the employees stop respecting their manager. In fact they now see their manager as a road block in their career development and advancement. The feelings toward this ineffective manager now transfer over to the company in general.

What's happened here is leadership development does not exist, employee engagement has been killed and innovation has stopped. The company does suffer and the employees will start leaving over time.

Let me tell you my personal experience with this as an employee. In the early 1980's I had become an employee at global investment banking company. When arriving there I was filled with enthusiasm and drive. My goal was to never work at another firm and to take over the world. Soon after arriving I was rising at a meteoric pace. I was performing at level, that by any metric applied, the employer had never seen before. My direct manager was a guy who had been there for 25 years. During this time I arranged for the venture funding of the first Bio-Technology Company in the world. I arranged for the initial public offering of one of the first Health Maintenance Organizations (HMO) in the country. I designed and implemented a cash management system for the excess treasury funds at some of the largest companies in the mid-western region of the U.S. This had never been done before and I was literally printing money, profits, for the company at unheard of level. Continually during this time I would go to my manager to tell him what I was doing and to get his approval. Each and every time I was met with his answer of, "I'll get back to you". In each case he would never got back to me so I would find a way to do it anyway. Here was the problem, in some cases there was no way to proceed without his approval do to the procedures that required it. In the situations that absolutely required his approval the answer was always the same, "I'll get back to you". I would try and try again and each time I would explain the large amount of money that the company would make. Even though I had high value from the perspective that my ideas had produced results in a tangible way and as such I had credibility, the response was always the same. I had reached a level of success in the industry such that even our competitors respected me and sought my advice. At one point a Director at a competing company had even contacted me and asked me, if they brought together their employees would I present to their employees on how to be successful. I did not ask for approval this time and I agreed to do it. I knew my manager would either not decide at all or on the rare chance that he did make a decision, it would be no. He would think why strengthen our competitor. I knew that if I were in front of them and approachable some of their best people might want to come work for us. I did the presentation, I was right and within one month five of their people joined us. After three years of "I'll get back to you", I wondered how much business we were losing. It was clear my manager was weak and ineffective. His boss was his best friend which allowed me no avenue to go around him. He was a protected employee. One fateful day I had gone back to my office in frustration. When I entered the room the phone rang, it was a headhunter. He let me know that the CEO of a competing firm wanted to meet me and I agreed. I hopped a plane to New York the next Monday and met with the CEO. He said, that he thought I was growing bored and frustrated with the road blocks put in place by my own company. He somehow knew this and he was right. We made a deal on that very Monday afternoon. I flew back that night and tendered my resignation the next morning. Both my boss and his boss were floored. They offered to change things if I would stay but it was too late. I remember thinking to myself, do I need to quit every time I needed them to decide on something. They had broken my passion for and belief in the company. Their inability to show leadership had driven me to their competitor. The competitor now had my ideas and the results going forward that my old employer had taken for granted. For me it was not about the money, my compensation was the same, it was about the environment of leadership and personal accomplishment.

What failed in this example and what fails at most organizations is week middle management that does not understand leadership development which leads to the high employee engagement that results in continual innovation. The lack of these things not only led to innovation stopping on my part, it led to me quitting and going to their competitor. Within a few years the company I left was no longer in existence and the company that I went to, is to this date, one of the largest financial institutions in the world.

Leadership

Are true leaders born not developed, some would say yes. I believe it's both. Most people have some leadership skills deep within them if the environment is right for it. Remember, what I said earlier, that a title alone does not make you a leader. A title may give you the authority to dictate orders to your subordinates but that alone is not the type of leadership that we are talking about here.

A true leader is trusted, admired and respected by their subordinates. This is earned leadership not dictated leadership. A true leader lives their leadership role. It shows up in every aspect of their lives. It's a way of thinking and a way of acting, not sometimes, all of the time.

Leaders don't place blame they take responsibility. They take action to make things better. If that takes changing a course that they themselves set in place, they do it.

The single most important thing that a leader does is expect, demand and encourage leadership growth from every employee they have regardless of the position of the employee. This isn't once a week or once a month, it's every day, all the time. They use plain language with all of their employees as to this leadership expectation. Leaders know that words without actions are worthless words. They take action that is tangible and visible to everyone.

They set in place an environment where every employee has to personally be part of the leadership process. Not just a part of the audience but a member on the stage. They understand that employee engagement in this leadership development process is part of getting the employees to embrace what they do. Regardless of the employees position they have to be part of the planning process and the presentation of those plans to their fellow employees. This is not hard to do and it will lead to the employees having ownership in the success of the organization. The employees who "want" to do something versus "having" to do something will excel at what they do and as a result be more productive, fulfilled and happier.

A leader does not see their rising star employees as a threat but instead sees them as a success of their own leadership skills.

I saw a middle management leader require all of his employees to take public speaking lessons. This is something that I believe in as a leadership building activity. In that I found someone who also thought as I did I asked him if his employees regularly had to do public speaking as part of their jobs. He said, "no, but it makes them stronger as an individual and gives them more confidence and pride". I asked if he was ever concerned that the employees might use this new skill and confidence to move to another company. His answer was quick, "If they do they do but they won't". I had asked him why he was so confident in their not leaving. His answer was right, that they respected and trusted him. They knew he took every opportunity to make them better people and better employees. This alone was not the only activity that he had put in place and on a whole these activities led his employees to love their jobs. The turnover in this managers division was virtually zero. His once back water, obscure division of the company had become the single most profitable part of this billion dollar company. The employee engagement had risen to such a level that virtually all of the innovation of the company emanated from his division. The senior executives of the parent company viewed his division as the new growth engine and future of the company.

I originally met him when he had called me to ask if I would speak to a large group of his junior managers on how to think and act like entrepreneurs. I had now become part of his continual daily efforts to make his team stronger. He additionally had asked me to speak on how to continually develop the leadership skills amongst all of their employees.

This leader got it and it was working. By strengthening every employee he was unleashing his human assets. His employees never left. I was told after my session with them that they were all trying to get their friends jobs there. Think about this for a moment, not only were they not leaving, they wanted their friends to be as happy and as fulfilled as they were. One asked me for my card and he said that they would walk thru fire for their manager. This is a moment of great importance. During the session I had asked the group if they could tell me what had made them the biggest, most profitable part of the company. There was a lot of laughter at the question but one individual looked around the room smiling and said, "It's because we do the impossible".

The manager had built the skills and leadership within his teams and each of these people had done the same within their teams. This esprit de corps had flowed thru the entire organization and become a way of life. In the process the employees grew to admire, respect and trust their respective managers and this respect now flowed all of the way up to the head of the division.

This very moment of importance is what allowed the managers to lay out the plans and goals, that all had participated in, and then ask the employees to do the impossible.

You do the impossible because you "want" to do it not because you "have" to do it. Leaders know this.

The employees want to feel important and they want to be part of something important. This Division manager had accomplished this.

Once the manager had brought the employee teams to this level of leadership excellence and engagement anything becomes possible. Innovation explodes which is the life blood of a company's future.

Leaders know it's important to make the goals big and challenging. They use that plain language mentioned earlier when stating the goal and the time frame. Most importantly, they state this, "It's not going to be easy". They also let the employees know, that they, the manager knows the employees can do this. Finally, at this point the leader "asks" them to do it, are they in and then waits for the reply.

Remember the employee earlier, that when asked why they were so successful, said it's because they do the impossible.

I cannot state this strong enough, you must ask not tell the employees to join the cause to achieve this record, almost impossible goal. It's imperative that it be their personal decision. Only in this way are they all in. If you wait for their answer, they will give it to you. This is that awkward moment of silence wherein he who speaks first loses. No matter how long it takes, wait for the answer. Remember, you've just asked this incredible team of new leaders to join you in this quest. One will respond, "I'm in", and the rest will follow immediately. You now have crowd commitment and full engagement.

The power of wanting to versus being told to cannot be overstated. Great leaders know how to get this level of commitment. They have all become leaders and now have one cause. They have made a personal commitment and are part of a group that has done the same. They are important, what they do is now important and they are now involved in something big. This will become infectious and will go viral throughout the organization.

NOW LEAD, INSPIRE and WIN

So many companies think employee satisfaction starts and ends with compensation, benefits and employee picnics. All I can say is, good for them. They can continue to deal with turnover, low morale and lackluster performance. Employees who are not part of something big are unhappy, unchallenged and looking around for other employment. They are unfulfilled and as such unhappy. This type of company does endless employee reviews and employee satisfaction surveys. The surveys claim to be anonymous but most employees don't believe it, so they don't give honest answers. Even if they answer honestly the remedies just do not address the lack of inspiration that exists.

In the first company used in this example they were willing to walk thru fire to accomplish the impossible and are proud to do it and want to do it. The satisfaction of these employees goes well beyond compensation and benefits. They are part of a great quest that makes what they do and who they are special. These people don't have to go to work on Monday, they want to go to work.

Now if you think this company must not be real or that they are working on something exciting like a new life saving medical breakthrough or perhaps something big like putting a man on mars, you're wrong. The company in this example is real. They make and sell agricultural products. So you have no excuse. What they have is a way of thinking and a way of acting. Leadership is not something they occasionally talk about. It's a way of life that they act on every day. Inevitably if there are employees who don't engage this process, then they are let go. There can be no room for anchors on a team that is on the move. This letting go of the uncommitted and nonbelievers is not a negative. It only reinforces and confirms in the remaining employees how special they are.

I must give another example of one more company that I worked with that I would tell you is one of the worst forms of leadership that I have ever seen. The company is real and sadly their idea and method of leadership is not isolated.

When I first got involved I asked the senior person what was their style and belief in leadership development. The answer was one word, "fear". Their methods and the environment they created had all employees feeling that they could be fired on any day of the week and without warning. The employees were reviewed for performance every week or two and without warning as to when the review was even going to occur. It was called, "the tap on the shoulder". It goes like this, while the employee was working, whether on the phone or in a meeting, they would be approached and tapped on the shoulder. The tap meant immediately stop. Leave the meeting or hang up the phone and proceed immediately to your manager's office for the review. If you needed to review some notes you were berated. If you hesitated in your answers for even seconds you were berated. Similarly, if all your answers were immediate, correct, and concise you were berated. When I asked senior management why this approach, they explained that all employees are week and dishonest at their core. Further, they said that employees who fear for their jobs every day of every weak will perform better out of this fear. In larger employee meetings, management would pick out one employee and verbally attack and berate the employee in front of the other attending employees. Management's idea here was that it created public humiliation and hence fear amongst all in attendance.

Needless to say, employee morale was at zero. Employee sense of mission and wanting to succeed was at zero. This company had operations across the U. S. and no one was immune given their various locations. The employee turnover was at almost 80% per year. The creation of new products and innovation was at zero. I can sum it up by saying, when an employee let me know they were leaving I would congratulate them. They would tell me that they felt finally free, like getting out of prison. When I would ask the departing employees if others felt this way, they would say everyone does.

Management was unmovable in their opinion on how to lead and manage.

None of the employees were invested in this company or its future let alone its success. This company's growth had been stagnant for years. I believe, their still existence was due only to the enthusiasm of new employees coming in each month until their spirit was eventually broken and then another group of new employees would arrive to replace them. The cycle would just continue on and on. Every employee who came into this business wanted to do well and make the company better and every one of them eventually left. I can only imagine the success this company would have if they turned off the fear and intimidation environment and turned on the leadership environment.

The leadership in this company was in title only.

A leadership based environment usually starts at the top but the idea of creating this type of environment can begin somewhere within middle management. If not starting at the top than it will need to eventually be sold to the C-Suite. Under any event it has to be embraced by the top leadership within the organization at some point.

Once the top person in the organizational chart "buys in", that individual needs to insure that it now becomes the new standard of operation. It starts with that top person declaring to the entire inner circle of management that the new initiative is in place and there is no exception, no debate. There has to be total buy in or it won't work. Any of the top echelon who don't embrace it and act on it will need to be let go regardless of their individual respective position or responsibility. It's that important to the success and innovation of the company.

In larger companies there is a Chief of each important part of the company such as Chief Executive Officer, Chief Operating Officer, Chief Revenue Officer, Chief Technology Officer, etc. Depending on the size of your operation this list can go on and on. I would propose you designate the Chief Leadership Officer to insure the new leadership environment is actually developed and acted on. It could be a person who also has additional duties and responsibilities in addition to this. Either way you need to designate the person in charge of the effort or it won't happen.

Be careful to take this action. If you don't, it will be a casual effort that will eventually be lost and abandoned as the daily pressure of business takes precedence over developing the internal leadership of the company.

Your goal is simple, propel your business by unleashing your human assets. The method to achieving the goal is to drive a leadership development way of acting and thinking through every single employee of the company.

The way to start this, with specific examples, will be covered later. I want you to know that once you start this process you'll see an immediate change in the company. You'll see the mood change in the first day if the employees sense that it's real and not just more words that have no meaning. It will occur if the words are immediately followed by action in the same day.

Unleash Your Human Assets-Getting Started

The unleashing of your people to propel your company or organization requires that certain ground work be laid. As the ground work is being developed, it needs to be followed up with by specific actions to create an environment that leads to the full engagement by the employees in the company. This will result in improved performance, innovation for the future and leadership. Take this step by step as follows.

1. Make the decision

I mean really make the decision and make it mandatory. Like parachuting out of an airplane you need to step out of the comfort and safety of the airplane and know it's now too late to go back. It's irreversible and there cannot be any in between.

2. Assemble the inner circle of management

Declare the new direction of the company. Explain that the company is now going to become the best place in

America to work and the best place for customers to do business. Not one of the best places the best place. Explain that the new initiative will drive leadership development to every employee in the company, it will create an environment of engagement by all employees and explode innovation. Explain that they, the inner circle of leadership, must embrace this and act on it daily or leave the company. You now have their attention. These are powerful words but they must know that this is serious. They must know that this will affect them personally and each and every employee. Now, ask each one if they are in and wait for their answer. Silence here on your part is your friend. Their either in or their out.

3. Pick the person who is now in charge, the new Chief Leadership Officer

Announce that you now have one month to put in place the actions that will create the environment that will unleash your people. This will be the daily and weekly activities, actions and responsibilities that all employees and their managers will participate in. Explain, that if this is done correctly the employees will "want" to do their jobs versus "having" to their jobs. Explain that there will be one person in charge of insuring that this is followed thru with. This is the Leadership Officer. In creating this structure with specific methods and activities you can use the examples in this book and additionally the other fine books on the subject that are available. The Chief leadership Officer needs to own this new way of thinking and acting first and then spread it down thru each layer of management and the general employees. Explain very clearly that creating the want to environment versus the have to environment requires that all intimidation, threats of termination for no reason, holding back or blocking star employees and all other company politics is to end immediately, as in right now. Explain that any management that cannot do this will have no future in the company. Explain, you want employee turnover to drop to as close to zero as possible. Explain that the result of the new employee enthusiasm and satisfaction must lead to all customers wanting to do business with your company. Note, the impression most of your customers have of your company and its products is directly related to the enthusiasm and positive nature of the employee they are dealing with. Explain, that without continual innovation your company will die and that the new environment will make your company the most innovative company in your industry. Explain that all innovation comes from the people and the people must want to innovate versus having to innovate. Be patient here, this one thing, "wanting to" versus "having" to environment is repeated here over and over again because it's the key result of leadership development. You need to focus on this and repeat it yourself over and over again and to everyone in the organization until they get it.

4. Creating a Leadership Environment

With the inner circle of leadership now in, bring in all layers of management into the conversation. Explain and state the items and goals listed in 1 thru 3 above. Explain clearly that they must learn and act as a leader on a daily basis or leave the company. Again, powerful words but they also need to realize how important this is and how serious you are. One non committed manager can and will weaken the entire effort. Explain this, that their personal success or failure will be determined by how they empower their people, lead their people and develop leadership within every employee, not just their favorites that answer to them. Let them know that they will become the leadership teachers themselves thru every interaction they have with every employee they meet with and without exception. If they are doing it right than it will be expected that their employees will be promoted over time and in many cases promoted to areas of the business outside of the manager's supervisory control. They are to develop the leadership skills within all of their employees such that some of these employees could take over the manager's job. You will get some resistance on this. A true leader does not fear replacing themselves in that they know by doing this they themselves will move up the ladder and have more responsibility. Remind them that holding back employees from advancement is forbidden.

 5. Employee Leadership Skill Development Employee Trust in Management.

Each manger now needs to lay the ground work for the activities and leadership development that will follow. This ground work is the establishment of mutual trust between the employees and their manager. This can be done in different ways but it's important that it occurs every day. I would recommend you start in this very simple way, you bring it up in the next staff meeting. Unlike other weekly staff meetings where a number of things are covered make this the only point of discussion for the meeting. Little things will matter here that will let the employees know that this is different. If you normally stand then do it sitting down. If you normally have notes then have no notes. Start by telling the employees that you want to make the company better by making them better. Tell them you cannot do it alone and in fact you can only do it if they help you. Let them know that you their boss want an environment of honesty that will go both ways and that you'll never let honesty hurt an employee and their career and that they have your personal word on this. Let them know that you will always strive to be honest such that they will never have to wonder what you really mean and what is really going on. Make this meeting relaxed and very conversational in nature.

Now you need to follow through on this with little subtle things that you'll do. Over the next week or two what will happen is what happens in every organization. The employees will come to your office door for various reasons. If they have an idea, take the time and listen to it. If it's a great idea let them know it and tell them good job. If it's not a good idea, let them know why in some detail versus just dismissing it and then thank them for coming up with new ideas whether or not it's a good idea. If they tell you they have no PTO left but would really like to leave two hours early on a Thursday to attend their child's school event. Tell them okay and maybe add that family is important and you're glad that their doing this. If you haven't told them this for a while maybe let them know you really like the way they handle themselves around the office and you think they are doing a good job.

What you're doing here is starting to develop a mutual respect relationship between the manager and the employees. These type of things may seem trivial and unimportant but they are not at all. You should carefully strategize a way to do this with each employee over the course of a couple of weeks prior to setting up the leadership activities. All of this is telling the employees that you are approachable, nonjudgmental, listening, supportive, appreciative of their efforts, aware of their accomplishments, fair and strong not weak. You value them. Just this will start to spread. Don't kid yourself, when you do this the employees go back and share with the other employees how well you treated them and how good you made them feel. They'll go home and share it with their spouse and friends. This is not weakness its strength and the employees will see it as strong not weak. There will be days when it's necessary to say no to a request but they will understand because of this relationship of respect and admiration that is developing.

In the weekly staff meetings where the manager normally does 80 to 100% of the talking fold in the employees such that they are doing half or more of the talking. Do this by asking certain employees what they think about the subject matter or ask them, if they've recently had some success and what was working for them. Again, your showing them that they matter, are valued and deserving of recognition. Remember, this is about building respect and admiration. These little things are actually big things in the eyes of the employees.

Equally important here is that this becomes your new way of acting on a daily basis. Not just at the weekly staff meeting but every day with every employee and with every interaction.

Your words are not empty if followed by tangible action.

In 3 above we stated, create the activities, actions and responsibilities that will occur every day to develop leadership skills for all employees. The initial list you come up with does not need to be all inclusive, it will change and grow over time.

Here are some suggestions that work.

Public Speaking.

Have all employees' right down to the lowest level employee take public speaking lessons. Have all of these employees then make a public presentation from time to time to the other employees on real issues involving the business or as will be discussed later a project that is being worked on. I know some of the readers here may be laughing at this point or thinking my employees job description does require public speaking or presenting to other employees. That's not the point. The point is building leadership skills and as a result building the confidence of every employee. It further gets the employees to take ownership in the item or project that they are presenting. Some employees will resist this. They'll say their nervous, uncomfortable and maybe afraid. Some may flat out refuse to do it. These are the very reasons they need to do it. It's okay, tell them everyone is nervous but their skills will grow over time and they will be a stronger person. Tell them it's not about passing or failing, it's about building confidence, leadership and skills over time. This activity will absolutely show tangible activity toward building leadership. Remember, words without tangible action will have no value to the employees. So show them action that involves them on a personal level.

As a case in point, I attended an event in the spring of 2015 in which the than Chief Executive Officer of Wells Fargo was the key note speaker. What he had accomplished in his career was the stuff of legends. He did not come from wealth and the connections that come with a blue blood upbringing. No, he grew up in a small remote town with a population of just 300 people. He came out of a small college and went to work at the bank. He had gone from this farm kid to being the CEO of one of the largest and most powerful banks in the world. He was asked at the end of his presentation on future innovation, what if anything was the one thing that led to his great personal success. With no hesitation he said the one thing was taking public speaking lessons. He said it was the one thing that taught him leadership skills and gave him the confidence to personally be a leader.

Reports.

Have the employees, not the managers, evaluate the necessity of some of the reporting. I'll explain this thru an example below.

Reports, have become the life blood of corporations. Overtime all organizations add reports on reports. In some cases no one currently at the company can tell you who originally started a specific report and why. It's something they have been doing for years. I consulted for six months with a national company that was a well-known service provider in their industry. Moral amongst the employees was horrible. They were zombie employees showing up to just get a paycheck. No energy, no creativity and no enthusiasm. The employees had never been presented an environment that made them feel like they were part of the decision making process in the company or that their opinions actually mattered. Reporting in this company had grown over time such that the average employee spent roughly 2 hours a day filling out reports. This left them with 6 hours to actually do the job they were hired for.

Some reports are necessary but the bulk of these reports were really meant to just document that the employees were doing their jobs. This was a huge waste of time and only led the employees to feel like they were not trusted. It was like a set of handcuffs. I evaluated the necessity of the various reports myself but instead of simply making the decision I decided to make the employees part of this process. I decided to empower them which had not been done before.

Here I saw an opportunity to build employee engagement, trust and leadership building. Even though their final recommendations were virtually the same as the decisions I had made it wasn't as important as the process to get there and the subsequent results that went beyond the reporting. It was important to give the employees a voice, to show them that we trusted and valued their analysis and that we wanted their leadership.

They knew the goal was as follows, make the company better and increase their productivity by evaluating the necessity of all of the reporting that had accumulated over the years. A simple and uncomplicated goal. This was started with a meeting to each operating group of employees within the company. In the meeting each group was asked to pick two leaders from their group. The leaders were to collect information and lead debate on the information within their group. Those two leaders than presented their recommendations to their group manager. The decision was then made by the manager and the two group leaders together. This decision was than presented to the group employees in a meeting. This employee presentation was made by the two group leaders not the group manager. All of this activity created leadership development for the individual employees whose input now mattered and the two employee leaders of each group along with the department managers who all learned how to do this. The presentations included not only the reports that would no longer be done or in some cases simplified but also the reasons and logic behind it along with an estimate of time saved each week by the employees. The results of this very simple task was nothing less than staggering in its impact on the employees. From a purely functional standpoint the reporting went from on average 10 hours per week to 1 hour a week per employee. The increase in productivity is obvious. More importantly all of the employees had become part of making the company better. The two leaders of each group developed their own leadership skills. One of those leaders was eventually offered my job. I was a consultant at the time and as such a place holder for the position. The promotion was an example to all employees that anyone can advance when they step out and show true leadership skills.

This was the first time in the company's history that the line employees were asked to leave their cubicles and lead an effort on their own to make the company better. The ideas now started to flow from the employees on how to improve performance, increase sales and cut out wasted expenditures in many different parts of the business.

That day there was a constant stream of employees coming to my office door to share how excited and motivated they were. A few weeks later the employees organized a party, without input from management, to celebrate their accomplishments and the new company they worked for. The excitement and new sense of pride and accomplishment went viral. Within 4 months the revenue of this company doubled on a month over month basis. It doubled because the employees wanted it to. Their new enthusiasm and confidence was now flowing out to the customers and prospects of the company.

To this day the employees meet once a week, pick their leaders and choose an area of "their" business that they "want" to make better. This simple activity unleashed the human assets and propelled the company. Turnover dropped in half. In a note of humor, one of the reports they got rid of was the weekly report on whether all of their other reports were completed and turned in.

Remember, employees hear the words you say but will judge you on your actions.

The next example is of what was done to correct a horrible situation wherein the manager of a marketing department knew nothing about employee engagement and leadership development. You should use these methods and actions if you have a sales and marketing department.

Typically a marketing team operates in a bit of a vacuum. They do studies and perform research and then produce the message and collateral materials which are then given to the sales team to relay out to the customers as to why the customer should buy what the company is offering.

Here's what's missing though. I recently worked with a company that had beefed up its marketing department. This company produced intellectual property, content, that was then sold to the customer base. The marketing department would first tell the production department what content to create. The created products along with the message and marketing materials were then given to the sales people to take out to the market.

This company had marketing and production spend six months creating the new products and marketing materials. It was an all hands on deck, 24 X 7, half a year effort. The big day came, the sales team was assembled for the presentation of the new products. At the end of the presentation there was absolute dismay on the faces of the sales team. The room was silent for an awkward amount of time. At this point one brave sales person stated, "We talk to the customers and prospects all day long, this is not what they want to buy". She further offered, "Shouldn't we make and sell what the customers want". The meeting exploded into arguments. The sales people left and felt totally ignored. I spoke with a number of them later. They did feel ignored and that management placed no value in them. A few of the top sales people confided in me that they would keep doing their jobs but they were going to start looking around for a new job. They now questioned the long term viability of the company.

So many things happened here that were wrong. The first was that the head of marketing and the head of product design and production assumed they possessed all knowledge and would dictate to all subordinates what to do. The second is they disenfranchised all subordinates. They had destroyed all belief in the company. The spirit had been destroyed. I heard comments like, "Management were idiots". They were right. In addition to crippling the employee base, they had spent a half a year creating products that no one wanted to buy and no one "wanted" to sell.

Here's what I did and what I want you to do. The goal was simple, create products that the customers wanted to buy and create leadership, engagement and innovation throughout the employee base all at the same time. Time was not on our side.

I pulled all employees from the sales department, marketing department and production into one room. I explained that the solution needed to come from all of them not me and I needed everyone in the room to step up and show leadership. Remember statements without action will go nowhere. Here goes the action. The sales team was to meet immediately after the meeting. They were to pick two leaders of their group. They then were to develop a series of questions that each salesperson would ask the customers and additionally some prospects that were not customers yet. They had one week to call out to the market place and explain that we were doing the research to find out what the customers wanted and needed versus what we and the other competitors were providing. They were in addition to the phone call activity get in person meetings with as many people as possible. They were to explain up front that it was not a sales call but instead it was to get needed information from the customer base. They were to ask for the customers help. For the in person meetings they were to bring one member of the marketing team. The marketing person was there to observe only and hear the answers to what was important and needed by the customer. Up until this point the marketing people had never actually sat across from the customers.

After this week of activity all of the sales people were to meet again. The meeting was to be held by the two leaders who the group had chosen with one of them taking notes. This meeting did have two rules to keep it focused. Every sales person had exactly 5 minutes to present to the group the top three things that the customer stated were the most important things to them. In this case each sales person also heard from the other sales people what the important things were. The two leaders then compiled the three most important mentioned items and additionally the next three most often mentioned items.

The marketing team also had a meeting where they had to pick two leaders for this process. Note, in neither group was the manager to be one of the leaders. I'll explain why later. The marketing team at the end of the one week effort had to report in a meeting the same results that they learned in their in person interaction with the customers. The same rules applied, 5 minutes each and the top three items discussed by the customers. The two leaders compiled the information from their group.

The four respective leaders of both the sales and marketing teams then held a meeting with all of the members of the production team. The only rule here was to give the customers what they wanted not what we wanted. Discussion and questions were allowed by all of the members of the production team.

All of the members of the design and production team then held a separate meeting to discuss what they could produce per the customer's needs, at what cost and in what time frame. The only rule was hit the customers "bullseye". They had to pick two leaders of their group to lead their discussion and record the results.

The six leaders of the three departments were to pick a name for the project. In this real life example the name they chose was, "Hail Mary". The reason they gave for the name was they thought the project was big and not going to be easy to pull off.

Remember, earlier we said employees want to be part of something big, hard to achieve and important.

The six leaders then held a meeting with all of the employees of the sales, marketing and production departments to summarize what they could get done in getting the customers what they actually wanted and needed. In this case the production teams were going to have the new products done in 5 weeks. Marketing was going to have all marketing materials completed in 3 weeks. The sales team was going to start talking to the market place about the new products immediately. Senior management signed off on project "Hail Mary". The six leaders met once a week to report to each other the progress being made by each group to hit the deadlines.

Let's talk about what happened here. This project was created to fix a huge, possible company killing mistake made by a manager who did not understand leadership and leadership building. The marketing manager who created this problem quit two days after I announced the new initiative. The employees saw that as a positive and were excited to see her go. Though this process occurred to fix a problem you should do this for all new product development.

The results occurred as follows. All employees became part of "Hail Mary", their personal opinions and efforts now mattered, they were valued. All of these employees were engaged and now had ownership in the success of the company. The effort was big, important and not going to be easy. It made work exciting and challenging. In picking their six leaders they were making a decision and confirming in their own minds what qualities made those people leaders. To the six leaders it confirmed in each of them that they were viewed as leaders and what the qualities were that made them leaders. For the managers it was a tangible effort that led to engagement and leadership training for all of the employees. For the company it created the perfect scenario, leadership was developing, the employees were excited and doing what they wanted to do not what they had to do. For the sales department they now had the best products in the market and were excited to let the world know it. Another thing happened here that cannot be left unsaid. The customers now felt that they were important to this company. The customer's opinions mattered to this company and they also helped develop the best products in the market. The result of this was that the customers now became some of the best sales people for the products. The employees were now working for the best company in the industry and the customers were now doing business with the best company in the industry.

Banners were placed inside the hallways of the business that stated, "Hail Mary". Every employee received a plaque naming them as a member of "Hail Mary 2014". Each customer and prospect that contributed to the information gathering received a large plaque naming their company and thanking them for the design of the 2014 products. They were referred to as "Partner in Product Design".

As a side note the marketing manager was not replaced by a new person. The two leaders of the marketing team stepped up and asked if they could co-manage the department going forward. For them it was not about money it was about leadership and being part of something big going forward.

Leadership was now infectious.

Don't think that this is supplanting the managers. They have plenty to do, hiring, training and guiding along with all the other administrative task necessary to manage a department within a company.

Once you set up one of these activities and go thru the entire process it will become obvious on how to do this. The key will then become continually keeping it up. This absolutely creates a sense of satisfaction, fulfillment and loyalty within the employees. Your good employees are not going to want to leave this. They know it does not exist in other work settings or at best is very rare.

There are many examples of how to engage the process of developing a leadership environment. The key is to take tangible action or the words alone will have no meaning. Most of the companies I have interacted with say that they absolutely believe in leadership development and actively promote it. The truth is they don't. They say the words but they do not create the actions that make it real. The employees are hired, told by HR what a great place it is, trained and then shown their cubicle. Their manager comes out once a week to tell them what to do. This describes most companies in America and it begins the day to day process of the employees becoming bored, disenfranchised, disappointed and unhappy. They only do what they have to while they start thinking about looking for a new job. I think if senior management actually knew the real percentage of their employees who were unhappy and thinking of leaving they would, sadly, be very surprised. My guess and hope is that they would call a meeting and try to turn it around.

Mind Set

Your most valuable assets are your employees. They create the ideas, new products and innovation that will propel your company higher. Retaining your employees, developing your employees and getting their absolute best is all about the leadership that leads to your employees wanting to be their best and wanting to grow your company.

So many of the things we do have become so standard that we take them for granted. An example would be the Human Resource Department (HR). Look, I have nothing against the HR department, they also have to develop their leadership. Many companies put the burden of employee development and satisfaction on HR and they're simply not equipped to do it on the level and to the depth that were talking about here. Further, they do not have the departmental authority to accomplish it in a way that's meaningful. What comes out of HR in trying to create an employee happiness environment are things like birthday month, a listing of employee birthdays occurring during the month. Maybe it's the decorating committee for the holidays or planning committee for the year end party. To be blunt, these are the kind of things that are done for kids in a school. Certainly none of these activities are challenging and leadership building. Tell me of one great employee who won't leave because they helped decorate for the holiday season. The satisfaction and happiness of the employees is then measured via the employee satisfaction survey. No one who is unhappy, uninspired and unmotivated tells the truth on these surveys which makes the information completely useless. Seriously, stop doing them, they are a waste of both time and money.

The mind set to get this done needs to start at the top and flow through the entire organization. The idea to create a leadership driven environment can come from anywhere within the organization but it then absolutely needs to be sold to and embraced from the top.

The mind set were discussing here does not require more work on the managers part but it does require a commitment and set of talents that are somewhat science with a little magic thrown in. There are specific examples in this book that can be implemented in almost any setting. The manager needs to learn how to create and then implement very specific activities along with the delegation of group leaders to drive the project forward.

This can be done by simply picking either your own project or one in this book and then following the steps that are contained here. It won't be perfect at first and that's okay. If the commitment is there and your mind set is to focus and follow through on leadership development it will then get better and continually improve on a daily basis.

Identify the following activity categories, "crisis", "critical", "improvements" and "future initiatives". Have the employees, along with the managers identify individual projects or activities within each category above that will improve the company. Ask the employees to give a name to each project as discussed earlier. Giving it a name makes it real and tangible and it allows the employees to be attached to it and responsible for it. Other than management agreeing to the project and the time table for each, they are to get out of the way. This is the hardest part. The nature of management is to control everything. If you let this happen then don't start, you will fail.

Don't forget the goal, unleash your employees to propel the company higher and higher.

If you think your employees are not capable enough to do this than you should not have hired them. Managers who just cannot let this happen or view this as a threat need to be let go. It means they are insecure, authoritarian, controlling or just don't get it. The employees working for this type of manager will remain unfulfilled, unchallenged and unhappy. It will hurt your company's potential.

The hardest part of this process for management is the trusting of employees to pull off their part of this. This willingness to trust the employees is one of the single most important aspects that is absolutely required for this to work. I know that for some of you reading this you're thinking no problem. You're saying you can help pick a project, set out the rules of picking the leaders, time tables, etc. and then you'll step back. I want you to focus here for a moment. This is so easily said and yet so hard to do. Human nature is to tell others what to do. This is certainly amplified in the work place where there is a chain of command. The authority and chain of command absolutely stays in place but you need to let the employees drive the solutions to the problems and the methods to grow the company. This is the leadership development part that is necessary to create engagement and then innovation. If you don't do this then what you're really doing is micromanaging. Micromanaging is without question one of the top five reasons employees give for why they are leaving where they are at. It is actually the opposite of the mind set required to developing leadership. Micromanagers need to either stop doing it or be let go. The problem here is that it tends to be a personality trait and as such it is very hard to simply stop doing it.

Here is a case in point. I just spoke with a colleague who is the head of sales at a mid-size communications company. Her results at this company have been nothing less than impressive. Under her leadership the company has had back to back years of above industry growth. The company has done so well it is now merging with a larger competitor. The problem is that the company being merged with is larger in scope and as such she will still be running her group but she now has a new boss for the merged company. Though the agreed to plan is that she is to continue as before given her credibility via the results she has delivered, her new boss cannot stop himself from trying to micromanage her efforts. He is calling and emailing six times a day checking on her progress. He insists on seeing all customer presentations before they go out for his approval, with his approval being regularly late in the coming. He's not requiring that he see them because of a policy change or a change in how they are done, he's just micromanaging. She has proven her ability to develop leadership, engagement and innovation within her team but now a micromanager above her is going to drive her out because he cannot stop what he's doing and does not understand leadership.

She let me know she is going to leave her current employer. This is a person who is on a continual basis sought out by headhunters. My guess is that within a year of her leaving the bulk of her team will also leave and the upward growth of the company will end.

If this weren't true it would be funny. The larger stagnant company is in effect acquiring the smaller fast growing company to capture their growth. In the process the stupid micromanager of the acquiring company is driving out the single person who created the environment that has led to the growth. This is so important, you need to get this right.

A great leader facilitates leadership development within everyone they engage with. They know how to trust and then get out of the way.

Start with your own mind set and commit to this initiative, this way of thinking, this way of acting. Leadership will begin with you.

Reality is reality, at each step there are those who will nod in agreement but who are not really in. Get rid of them. This act alone will begin the entire organization understanding that this initiative is real, tangible and to be acted on. This will work.

"Visualize Yourself"

Ask yourself if you've ever met that manager or maybe a business owner who seems so relaxed. Everything just seems to be clicking for them. They're personally doing well and their company is doing well. They almost seem more like an observer to all of the innovation and performance going on all around them. Instead of coming in each day and having to personally push that heavy rock up the hill in an exhausting way, they come in and hear about all of the wonderful things that are occurring all around them. The employees who are updating them are happy and have a bounce and energy in their step. The mood of the entire place is positive with lots of smiling faces.

I want you to visualize yourself as this person. I want you to ask yourself if you would like to be this person and as such have their life versus perhaps the one that you have.

The difference is this person somewhere along the way created a leadership environment. They empowered their people, removed all of the handcuffs and then successfully got out of the way.

I want you to be this person, life will be good. Your employees will be happier, you will be happier and your family will be happier.

PERFECTION

A number of years ago I sat on the Board of Directors of a large consumer products company. Also on the Board was a fellow who's day job was being the Chief Financial Officer of a fortune 500 company. His company was the largest in the world at what they did.

After one of the Board meetings we had attended it was agreed that he and I would get together for the purpose of getting to know each other better. We sat down in a coffee shop and took a look at our respective calendars. The first date chosen started an eye opening conversation that went on for an hour. He said he could not make the first day chosen because he would be in the Rocky Mountains in a leadership training session. This particular event happened every two years and it was mandatory. Trying to make conversation, I asked if it was at a resort. Here it comes, "No", he said, the senior management were all flown out to the mountains, then led one by one into the mountains to remote locations. Each senior officer was left by the guide's miles from each other. There were no campsites, no tents, just enough supplies to support life along with a pad of paper and two pencils. There was plenty of water, a very small amount of food and a book of matches. They were left there for four nights and on the fifth day the guide's would return and take them out. The original routes into their respective locations had been disguised so as to discourage any thought that they might give up and just walk out on their own.

Along with surviving they were to use the paper and pencils to do two things. They were to identify new initiatives for the company and how to build leadership amongst all of the employees of the company. I said, it seemed dangerous, what if someone became injured. He said the guides would from afar observe them once a day on the rare chance that one of them had become injured. During the five days they each had no human contact, no cell phones, only the paper, pencils and the goal.

He had done this two years earlier and said it was probably the most valuable and interesting business experience he had ever had. He was more than willing to share what happened the last time he had done this.

He said the first two days they each basically wondered around, learned they could make a fire for warmth and ate the bulk of the food they had each been provided. In his case he was down to a few energy bars by his third day.

In the third day though he said something started to happen. Having been isolated with no human contact, no distractions of any sort, just the basic bare necessities of life had now allowed him to think freely about the goal. The pencils started flying across the paper with ideas. By the fourth day the flowing ideas and the writing was all that he was doing.

In his case the initiative that came out of it was that each departmental manager in their headquarters along with all C-Suite officers were to once a year be assigned to one of their thousands of branch offices. They were to be completely anonymous with no knowledge by the branch employees who they really were. They were to put on a smock which was the employee uniform, punch the time clock and do what they were told to do by the branch manager. The branch manager also had no idea as to who they really were. In that they had in excess of 20,000 branches the odds of being found out was very low.

He said everyone was involved from the HR managers, accounting managers, marketing, logistics, procurement, legal, IT, on and on. They moved boxes, ordered branch supplies, swept the floors and most importantly they dealt directly with the customers at the cash registers. They were to learn what the line employees actually did, what were their challenges and disappointments.

Along with learning the most basic functions of the business they were to learn the world of the employees and how to create tangible leadership development within them. He told me his original end goal in this was to reduce the relatively high employee turnover that they had which resulted in a high cost burden which they had to absorb thru having to continually be recruiting and training new employees. The other was to develop leadership that could move up in the branch system and manage the new branches being opened at a rate of 5 per day around the world.

The CEO became a believer in this process. He was one of those guys who woke up each morning with the goal of taking over the world. He wanted leadership development to occur from the lowest level employee up to the C-Suite such that no competitor could touch them.

He told me the results were as follows. Leadership teams had been established from the branch level employees all the way up to the C-Suite with no departments being exempt. The teams now develop and are in charge of their respective initiatives that can make the company better. Each initiative is given a name with a clear goal and a deadline. Being an old military officer, the CEO fully embraced this mission critical approach with every employee having ownership in the success of their named initiative.

It worked in a very big way.

Their employee turnover is now very low and they are now repeatedly voted one of the best companies in the world to work for.

Over the years they have acquired other businesses and then deployed this mind set into each one. Each of these businesses then became the leader in their industry.

Their logo and name, Federal Express, is now known throughout the entire world.

Wall Street loves them.

Competitors do chase them around the world but to date none have been able to catch them.

This company in the time frame of just a few years had gone from not being able to make payroll to being the biggest and best in the world. Their success came from valuing and believing in the employees and that every employee must have ownership in the success of the business. This all started with employee leadership on all levels.

What Failure Looks Like

Is this you? Like many things in life you need a benchmark or comparison to know how you're performing. The following are not necessarily bad things on their own but it begs the question, what else are you doing and is it enough.

Let's walk thru the typical steps that companies use to maximize the quality of the employees they pick and then what happens after that. Some of this may seem boring but it's meant to show how sanitized and boring we've made the process.

   1. Resume Screening

Resumes are screened thru software to see if enough of the right words that apply to the job description are contained in the resume that has been submitted. Many job descriptions have requirements that go beyond just specific technical skills such as an electrical engineering degree. Such that some of the traits sought are more like team player, leadership skills, etc. Every writer of a resume has the same number of words in the English language to choose from but if they did not pick the right words the resume is kicked out. This is a failure point.

2. Screening Calls

Talent acquisition staff members make a screening call on the submitted resumes that made it thru the screening software. Here they try to get in a 10 to 15 minute conversation a sense of whether the candidate is worthy of an initial interview with the hiring manager. The industry average age of a talent acquisition team member is 25 years old. Think about this, a person with virtually no real world experience is now going to determine if a candidate has the characteristics worthy of an interview. When Albert Einstein was applying for a position in school a staff member of the school wrote his parents rejecting him saying he was not bright enough and hence unteachable. The smartest person alive on earth was turned down by an unskilled person. This is a failure point.

3. Interviews and Testing

The future employee candidate has made it thru software screening and the screening call and now has an interview. There may be between two to four levels of interviews depending on the nature of the position. As a part of the process the candidate may take a test on technical knowledge and or a personality test.

    4.   The Candidate Now Turns Into an Employee.
They are highly motivated and filled with anticipation.

    5.   HR Now Has the Employment Agreement along with all necessary other documents signed.
HR congratulates the new employee and tells them what a great place the company is.

    6.   Training.
The employee now goes into training that depending on the position lasts between one to two weeks.

    7.   Work station.
Employee now shown their work station and begins to perform the repetitive nature of their job.

    8.   Quotas and Work Load are assigned.
Employee is told what they are required to produce each week and the reports to fill out.

    9.   Departmental Meeting's.
Department meetings are held once a week. Department Manager does 80 to 100% of the talking.

    10. Employee Reviews.

The employees manager does either a once a year or twice a year performance review of the employee.

11. Reporting
Employee fills out reports as to the meeting of their quota of the work assigned.

12. Employee Satisfaction Survey
Employee fills out the anonymous employee satisfaction survey but is less than candid for fear of retribution. Few employees trust that these are actually anonymous.

13. Starts Over Again
Manager works all over again with their HR partner to start finding replacement candidates for the prior employees who have left or are leaving. It is so assumed that the employees will leave that the process of finding the replacement begins before it's even known which employee is going to quit.

Does any of this sound familiar. Well in some cases there is more to consider.

1. Company pays competitive wages.
2. Company may offer pre-approved tuition reimbursement.

3. Company offers occasional promotions to fill the positions left open by departing employees.
4. Company offers a 3% to 5% raise.
5. Company pays for the employee picnic each year.
6. Company pays for a year end employee party.
7. If someone dies, gets fired or quits you may move up.

None of these things are bad on their own, but if this or something like it is all you do at your company than you have failed. Most of these procedures and or benefits were designed by some well-meaning person, perhaps HR, who has never been a leader themselves or has no understanding of leadership development. As stated earlier, none of these things are bad but they fall short of creating an environment that goes well beyond these most basic compensation and benefits needs. The message here to employees is, fit in, do your job and you will be compensated.

The personal satisfaction and happiness of an employee goes well beyond compensation, benefits and the little things like picnics. When most employees leave a company it is rarely about compensation and benefits.

This is what failure looks like. You're probably in business and profitable. But are you driving to be the best. No.

I'm sure when you were reading it you started to feel uncomfortable as you realized that it was your company. All of these things are necessary, it's just that there is so much more that should be done to energize, motivate and fulfill the employees and none of it involves more money.

Imagine now a sports team that took this sanitized approached to their employee players. They don't because they want to win. Every day, every week regardless of how they last performed they need to be their best at every practice and in every game. Every player has to have ownership in the single mission to win. This is accomplished thru leadership on and off the field. What the players are involved in is big and not easy to accomplish. All of the employee players are part of special teams within the team and each has its leaders. They win because they "want" to win not because they're "told" to win.

They know that just showing up is not winning. What's described at the beginning of this chapter is an environment that leads to just showing up.

Your employees are sick and tired of just showing up, they want to win. They want you to create an environment that unleashes them and leads to working at a winning company. They want the personal pride and satisfaction that comes from this. They desperately want to be engaged and filled with passion for what they personally do and for the company they work for.

Trust, Respect and Admiration

Who would not like being trusted, respected and admired, if only this were possible? It is possible and absolutely necessary if you're going to be successful. In other places within this book you met real people who accomplished amazing results with their organizations. Each one of these people were just everyday people who earned the trust, respect and admiration of their employees. They knew, that to be able to ask their employees to do the impossible they needed to first accomplish this. Further, they knew that their title alone did not give them these things. They knew, that for the employees to actually work on accomplishing the impossible, when asked, it required these things.

You can tell your employees to succeed, you can order them, you can threaten them with consequences if they don't succeed and yes you can even ask them to succeed but without the employees trusting, respecting and admiring you the extra effort required to succeed will not occur.

Smart managers are well thought out and intentional in how they earn this from their employees. They know it cannot be halfhearted or phony.

The employees obviously know you're their boss. They know you can decide whether they can get a promotion some day and conversely they know you can demote or even terminate them if you choose. Regardless of these actions that they know you can take regarding their future, what they really want are the reasons from you such that they can trust you, respect you and admire you. This is what they want and it's there for your taking, all you have to do is earn it. Know this, it's the number one reason for employee job satisfaction.

After you've earned these things you then need to be able to inspire them. I know this may seem beyond some of you to accomplish this. Perhaps a little over whelming given all your other daily duties or maybe it's just not who you are given your personality type. Understand this, if you're going to be the boss and as such succeed at getting your team to do the impossible, it's mandatory that you achieve this with the employees. Your organization that made you the manager needs you to do this. The employees that answer to you desperately want you to do this. Look, not everything is for everybody. I want you to think really hard here as to whether you're a person who can earn these things from your employees. Whether you're willing to do what it takes on a daily basis to achieve this. If the honest answer is it really is not you, then you need to let your superior know this. There is no hiding when the organization is driving at full speed toward success. If your honest answer is yes, you can do this and that you are committed to doing this then make a conscious decision that this is now who you are. Anything less will lead you on a path to failure.

We'll now fold in some examples of exacting things that you can do. Some of these things may seem trivial to you at first but they are not. In the eyes of the employees it's the accumulation of the many little things that you do, that matter to them and how they view you.

The order of these things starts with trust first. Once you've established employee trust in you it then moves next to respect for you. Now that there is trust and respect established it moves finally to admiration in you.

These things go both ways though. I hear it all the time, unhappy employees saying, my boss has no trust in me. Hence they are unhappy and feel unappreciated. To get your employees to start trusting you than you need to show them first that you trust them. Begin here first and start showing your trust in small tangible ways. Micro managing on your part or constantly checking on progress or telling the employee how to do every little detail of their job is not trust. I have never met a hard core micro manager who admitted that they do this. They're usually shocked and in disbelief when it's brought to their attention that they do this. Instead, try this, after the project or goal has been established then tell the employee that you have absolute confidence in them to get it done or pull it off. Maybe add the following, which if they have any questions or need help to just ask. This may seem like a small nuance that you think should just be assumed but by saying it you've now just shown them that you trust them.

When an employee comes into you with a question on something, do not just give them an answer on how to do it. Instead, ask them to tell you the issues and then ask them what they would recommend or what ideas they may have. You're telling them that you value and trust their opinion. Again, this may seem small but the employee will leave with a smile and they will tell the other employees that you wanted their opinion.

Occasionally pick one of your employees and ask them to spend a few minutes with you. Tell them you were just thinking about all of the moving parts of the office, projects and maybe some of the things discussed in the weekly staff meetings. Now, shock the employee by asking him or her if they think anything is being missed. Let them talk without interruption, listen to their thoughts and ideas. When they're done commenting, thank them and end by saying that you trust and value their opinions.

Think of something that is minor in consequence and that is specifically against an unimportant company policy that you know everyone is aware of. Some examples might be someone asks for the onetime event of coming in one hour late on a certain day. Or maybe they ask if one of their kids can come in for just two hours, one time, in that there is no one to watch them at that time. Maybe it's that the company policy is not to each lunch at one's desk. There will be a myriad of things that you'll be able to think of that apply to your business. Again, these are small things. What you're going to do here is let the employee win when you don't have to. You're going to break the rules that don't matter. When the employee comes to your office to explain and ask for this favor, look them in the eye, maybe give them a smile and say no problem. Add the comment that you trust them and that you never worry about them abusing the rules. Again, you're showing trust in this employee. These employees know that you're doing something that you don't have to do but you're doing it anyway and you're doing it for them. You're showing them that you're relaxing the rules because you value them and you trust them.

I know that these little gestures may seem trivial to you. These little weekly things add up quickly though and the impact on how the employees start to view you and trust you is quite significant.

Always stick to your word with your employees. Make a practice of making your word your bond as it applies to the employees and something you either told them they could do or that you would do. It's imperative to do this even if after some later reflection you either don't want to do it or can't do it. The employees need to know and become used to how solid your word is. This tells the employees that they can count on you.

Always tell the employees the truth even if the truth hurts you. They won't look down on you for this, they'll see it as strength and honesty. They will now trust you and respect you for this. This one act now tells them that they also can tell the truth because they trust that you also won't look down on them. There can never be punishment for truth telling. It's the core of trust.

Keep your door open, carry yourself well and with confidence and always listen. In fact do much more listening than talking. You are their leader so pick your words carefully, always be just and fair, never dictatorial or selfish.

They want to trust you, respect you and admire you. Now, this will start to happen and grow daily. Overtime as new employees come in, the older employees will let them know what a great leader you are and that you are to be respected for who you are. Your way of acting will make them admire you and also teach them on how they can be the same kind of person. Your team is now developing into a group that strives to be the best people that they can be.

When the Passion is Gone

So when does the employees passion for their job end. Like anything it's different for each employee. As mentioned in a previous chapter it will happen at the majority of all companies. It does not have to happen though.

For virtually every new employee coming into a business, they enter filled with excitement. We know and it's widely documented, that the majority of all employees are unhappy in their respective jobs. This has proven to be true regardless of the level of the position. It must be asked then, why do they come in so excited and then become so unhappy and disengaged.

I've heard managers explain this away in a number of ways. They'll say the position has high turnover do to the mundane nature of the job itself, or in the reverse they'll say the position is high pressure, high demands and it burns the employees out. The extreme I've heard is that there just are not any good people to hire so they get the bottom of the barrel. Further, that these employees are lazy, untrustworthy and unreliable hence the high turnover. What they never say, is, it's our fault that they leave.

Remember earlier we said that words without tangible action are worthless. I get such a kick out of employment ads that say things like "high pace", "challenging", "advance your career", "be part of an exciting environment" and "rewarding". These are all empty words and we all know it. To add insult to injury somebody came up with the idea that all companies need to come up with a public statement as to the companies "commitment to employees". They'll spend weeks and months coming up with these words. They'll print it, frame it and then proudly display it in the lobby of their business. Does this sound familiar, perhaps it's your business. Let's face it, these are empty words.

What if we told the truth in the employment ad or in the commitment to employees such as "competitive wages, repetitive mundane work and a non-motivating, uninspiring environment"? We can't tell the truth or no one good would work there. So instead we lure them in knowing the good ones will leave eventually.

Once the employee's passion is gone it really is too late. They'll do what you or I would do. They'll do the bare minimum while they are secretly looking for a new job. They'll put out feelers with friends and contacts. They'll start searching job sites at night and on weekends. They'll start using up their vacation and sick days going to interviews. Understand this, they did not fail in their jobs, the company failed them. Why spend so much time and money to recruit, hire and train the best you can to than allow a situation that you control, wherein the result is the best will eventually leave. Don't kid yourself they will leave.

In the exit interview most people are kind and just want to get it over with. They'll say something like, "I love all the people here", or "I'll miss everyone but I found an opportunity I can't turn down". What they won't say is, "this place is uninspiring". After all, why burn a bridge, why say the truth, nothing is going to change anyway. What you should ask yourself, is why they were looking to begin with.

The employee who joined the company originally did not have as a goal to quit the company when they first started. On the contrary they came in with excitement, anticipation and a desire to be inspired. Just like the company does not want to continually be finding new employees to replace the ones who have quit. The employee also does not want to have to go look for a new job. It's time consuming, disruptive and expensive to both parties. So they each have this in common, yet it keeps happening.

Most employees seek and would be more than happy and fulfilled with the below environment. Many companies can claim they have some of these things but few have all of them.

1. Well paid.
2. Appreciated and recognized.
3. Listened to.
4. Promoted.
5. Involvement in the decisions.
6. Mentored by their leader in becoming a leader themselves.
7. Respect, trust and admiration for their leader.
8. Challenged.
9. Inspired.
10. Being personally part of something important.

To simply say, your environment provides the first few items, is not enough though. The employee can get those things somewhere else. It's the second part of the list that leads to fulfillment and success for both the company and the employee. It's the second part of the list that requires leadership.

Remember, the employee will hear your words but they will judge you on your actions.

You can see the employees who are actually quitting when it occurs. Now, try to think of how many other employees, for each one that quits, that are only doing the minimum required to keep their jobs. Could it be 25% or 50% or even more that are unhappy. These are your zombie employees who have lost their passion. It absolutely affects the innovation and performance of every aspect of the business.

Everyday Leaders
"Exceptional Results"

There are those people out there who get it and as such they live a life of leadership on a personal level. They use every interaction they have with their employees to develop and build leadership within each and every employee they have.

Each of the people, who follow below, have used leadership development techniques to strengthen their respective organizations and then used that to propel their organizations forward. If you're like me you want more than just theory, you want real people with real results.

What should be of interest here and quite revealing is that each of these leaders came into an already existing organization. Each of these organizations had lackluster performance before their arrival. In each of their cases, after their arrival, employee turnover dropped, employee engagement went up and these companies exploded to the upside.

The question that one should ask is why they could achieve this and yet not one of their predecessors could. Other than their arrival nothing in these companies had changed. The employees were the same, the products were the same and the tools they had to work with were the same.

With this I would like to introduce to you these three gentlemen who are themselves exceptional.

Meet George Murray

I recently ran into George Murray over a cup of coffee. Let me introduce George. He is a humble and soft spoken man. In his mid-forties, married and with children. Early in his life he was a military man who exemplified commitment and sense of mission. He is a decorated Desert Storm/Gulf War veteran.

When George speaks his words are few but each well-chosen and with great impact. It's hard to get George to talk about himself in that he always talks about the people he has worked with and those that have worked for him when describing his success.

George has worked at a number of companies since leaving the military. In each of these companies his role has been an ever increasing position of leadership and responsibility. He currently is the Chief Operating Officer of a 100 year old company with operations around the world. In all of these companies there is one common thread. Prior to George arriving they all had lackluster performance, low morale and in some cases they were financially troubled. In each of these companies after George took the reigns there was an immediate and substantial increase in financial performance, increase in moral and reduced employee turnover. Each of these companies experienced a dramatic improvement in profitability.

His results are nothing less than impressive by any metric applied. In his career he has managed thousands of employees in numerous countries. He jumps across continents on airplanes and when he lands he deals with different languages, customs and currencies. Each time his results are the same, success.

When pressing George about why he's successful he'll only talk about the employees. For George it's not about him. He explains that the people, the human assets are who will take the company higher. He empowers the employees to each be leaders in solving problems and in improving the performance of the company. He lets every employee know they must always tell the truth even if the truth hurts them. Only in telling the truth can the company solve its problems and overcome the challenges. He lets them know they won't be punished or diminished for truth telling. It's the complete opposite, for honesty will only increase the value of the employee and their career growth within the company. George always shares the mission with employees. He lets them know in those few, well-chosen words, why what they each do is important to the success of the mission, that the mission is important in itself, not going to be easy and big. He gets them to acknowledge how important each person is to their part in the goal. He then asks them if they're in. He builds an esprit de corps wherein everyone works in the same direction to succeed.

George creates an environment such that the empowerment, leadership and success of his employees is his success. It's never been about George for he is a leader of people.

So, back to the coffee and where George is at now. Currently sixteen months into his newest role as the Chief Operating Officer of a company operating on three continents. When he arrived they were barely profitable, had no liquidity left on their balance sheet and moral was horrible. Spin forward sixteen months to our coffee meeting, after just sixteen months under George's leadership, profits had increased 83% and were the highest in the 108 years of the company's history, the balance sheet is flush with cash and they are returning money to the shareholders. Employee turnover is now very low.

It should cause thought as to why George Murray could accomplish in one year what his predecessors had not in 108 years.

What is the value of George Murray? I say it's priceless.

Meet Sam Taylor

So who is Sam Taylor? Sam is one of those people that even if you didn't know him you would still know when he entered the room that you were in. You would notice his steely eyed focus and when he spoke you would listen to every word. Sam is one of those natural born leaders that is able to develop leadership skills within everyone who works for him. Sam is the Chief Sales Officer of a now very successful software company. He is in his mid-thirties.

Where Sam goes big things happen. He fiercely believes in empowering his people and developing leadership throughout his organization. He has created an environment where his employees don't have to do their jobs, they want to do their jobs. They so value and trust Sam that they want to work for Sam and be where Sam is. Sam has created a place wherein he can ask them to do the impossible and they will do it. His employees don't go home from work, they go home and think about work. Simply put, Sam has created an environment where there is a sense of purpose, pride and accomplishment and it runs to every employee. When he first landed at his current company he moved immediately to get his employees to trust him thru the words he said backed up by the tangible actions he took. The sense he creates is that the employees are winners and they work for a winning team. Think about this, the sales division of almost all companies is where the highest employee turnover is. Under Sam's leadership there has been virtually no turnover. In Sam's words, "when one employee wins we all win together".

Sam believes that words with no action are words with no value. He knows that employees will hear the words you speak but that they will judge you on the actions you take.

For Sam, like other successful leaders, it's not about him, it's about the success of his employees. Sam works every day to strengthen the leadership within his employees and to create an environment wherein each one is engaged in the success of the company. Thru his direct actions the employees know this and it's why they want to work for him and why they'll go the extra mile to succeed.

He had a singular mission of getting the employees engaged on a personal level to make a run at accomplishing together the challenging goal he and his team had set. The goal was simple, explode the company to the upside. They were able to double the revenue of a 16 year old relatively stagnant software company in just a 15 month period. This occurred not due to a new product during this period, it occurred because he came in and empowered his people and then unleashed them. The employees did this because they wanted to not because they were told to.

So one should ask what works and what does not. Why was Sam able to do this in a matter of months and his predecessors could not in 16 years? It's called leadership and leadership development.

What is Sam Taylor worth to a company, I say priceless.

Meet Bill Titler

Bill Titler is a guy who makes every person he meets a better person. His conversations begin and end with just one thing, leadership, and winning. He so believes in this and practices it that every few words involves leadership. Bill will tell you though that words without tangible action are just words.

Bill is about 40 years old, married with children. He arrived at his latest company five years ago. The company had already been around for a number of years but had just not been able to break out of that one million dollar per year revenue level. Bill will tell you he saw potential but it would take building a team that no one could stop. The industry was highly competitive and as such unreliable price discounters were everywhere. After years of modest success, Bill knew the challenge would be large but he also knew that if the people were right and the leadership and environment were in place big growth could be had.

He knew their products and services were better than the price discounters so he changed the value perception of the products by raising the price and in some cases significantly. This is risky business but he knew he and his future team could differentiate themselves as to the higher quality and hence the higher price. He moved them from being viewed as a Timex to being viewed as a Rolex.

Bill went to work and started building his teams. What he looked for were people who if unleashed, could drive toward his implausible goals. Yes, he recruited, trained and motivated but he did much more than this. He connected with each employee on a deep level. He found each person's strength and gave them permission to be the best they could be, to be part of something big and to be successful. He let each team member know how big their task would be, how important they were as an individual to accomplishing it than asked each to make it happen. Bill knew that for an employee to accomplish the impossible they have to want to do it versus having to do it. Bill than removed all of their obstacles and handcuffs and let them run.

Again, like many successful leaders when discussing his personal success he almost exclusively talks about his people not himself. In the first 60 months of taking charge his team drove the revenue from $1,000,000 per year to $57,000,000 per year. The company's net profits now exceed the original revenue by tenfold.

Bill is a winner, his personal leadership and the leadership that he developed in each person allowed all of his employees to become winners. The goals he and his teams set were big and they were all part of making the impossible happen. Work had gone from being mundane to being exciting and a challenge that all wanted to participate in.

Is Bill smart, yes, in some cases perhaps the smartest guy in the room? Thru his leadership he was able to get his people to participate in and understand how to analyze the market they sold into. How to evaluate and then differentiate themselves from every competitor. In this process he was able to lift up his people to a leadership way of thinking that allowed each to be responsible for their own success and the success of the team.

Bill woke up one day and realized that his job there and his personal challenge were done. The team and the company had never been stronger. Knowing that what he had created was now sustainable he quit.

It's been about a year and this leader is looking for his next challenge where he can make a difference. Because of Bills personal success he doesn't need to work anymore, but he wants to. He wants to make a difference, he wants to beat all the odds. He's being careful, the company he chooses to work for will also need to understand leadership and will need to get out of the way of the tangible actions necessary for Bill to make it happen again.

To this day his old employees will call him to just let him know how well they are doing or to share how they just had a big win. They do this because they respect Bill and they know that he made this possible.

So what is Bill Titler worth to the right company, I say it's priceless.

Conclusion

Most companies and organizations that are doing relatively well believe they have covered all the bases and as such there really is not much more to do. Though they experience employee turnover it's accepted as simply the way things are.

The big question that's rarely asked is why this is occurring and is it necessary. So much has gone into hopefully hiring the right people and then so many leave each year anyway. There is a sort of musical chairs occurring in the world wherein employees leave your company to go to another company and yet employees will leave that company to come to your company. We know this is expensive on so many levels when dealing with recruiting, training and loss of momentum each time it occurs. The scariest part of this are the number of one's current employees who are just barely doing their jobs while they look around for another job. It's the lack of energy, momentum and lost ingenuity that's hard to measure.

So all of these employees that are moving around must be looking for something that they are not getting from their current employer. We know in most cases it has nothing to do with their current compensation level.

What's missing is true employee engagement in their organization which is the result of a lack of personal leadership development on all levels. Virtually all organizations use the words engagement and leadership but it stops with the words. There are no tangible actions that support or follow the words such that the leadership environment is real and with everyone personally participating in it on an everyday level.

Just the words without tangible action are just words that have no value.

As discussed, in this book, there are tangible actions you can take. The actions taken are not a distraction to the daily duties of each employee. It's the complete opposite. The positive returns for both the organization and the employees versus the time this takes far surpasses the effort. The employee turnover drops, while engagement, performance and ingenuity goes straight up. Everybody wins.

It begins with the managers establishing trust and respect from the employees. This is then followed by specific actions put in place that requires the employees to come up with the solutions and then they the employees act on making it happen. In this process the employees will learn leadership skills themselves. They will start to feel valued, empowered and important and as such start to take personal responsibility in the success of the project and the company. This is now full engagement. By doing this right you have in affect now given the employees permission to be their best with no handcuffs or stop signs in their way. This is how you unleash your people to propel your company higher. Ingenuity, innovation and revenue will increase.

This way of thinking and more importantly acting spreads thru an organization like wildfire on all levels. Unlike almost any other action an organization can take, this does not cost anything. This can be implemented without spending a nickel.

They will hear your words but will judge you by your actions.

All it requires is a decision to do it and then the right responsible team member who will insure that it occurs.

My nature is to be curious whenever I meet someone new. When it's a retired person and the situation at hand allows, I ask them where they used to work. The answer is almost always the same. Even though they had probably worked at a number of companies and or organizations, they always name just one. They don't go into their resume or list of six companies, they name just one. They then tell me it was the "glory years", the place they'll never forget. They'll tell me how they worked 60 and 80 hour weeks and loved every minute of it. They'll tell me it never felt like work, and it's the place that they grew the most as a person. They'll tell me how they worked on big things and made the impossible happen. They'll smile as they tell me how the boss they had was the greatest boss you could ever have. They'll tell me how they miss it. They feel this way because it was the place that made them feel valued and important.

You see, these employees desperately want to be inspired. They want to do the impossible. They want you to make this possible.

This is not an experiment with unknown results, it works. It gives your employees that one thing that they so desperately are seeking, the freedom and inspiration to succeed.

Finally, if you want your organization to win in a big way, unleash your people, your human assets, to propel you higher.

About the Author

Dan Shrader has been involved in the business world for 36 years. Having been rejected by a number Universities that he had enrolled at in the mid 1970's he attended the only college that had accepted him. He had no money but was committed to one thing which was a career in business and a business degree to help get him there. He made it thru college working two jobs at all times and a student loan for $600 for he had no choice but to pay for college himself. Within six years of graduating he was on the Board of Trustees of that same college and one of the largest contributors to the building of the college's new library. From poverty to wealth in six years. Immediately after college he accepted a position at a global Fortune 1000 company. In just a few months he realized there was little to do at this company, no challenge and no leadership to take him higher. He approached his boss with this problem and was told, that if he played his cards right he could maybe have his boss's job in 20 years. That night he thought, is this all there is and proceeded to turn in his resignation the next morning. He knew he needed more business knowledge and he decided it would come from

Wall Street. He applied at six Wall Street firms and within a month had received a rejection letter from five of them. With just one left that he had previously interviewed with he drove to their offices that Friday. He let them know he had interviewed at six firms and had decided to work at their firm. He further let them know that they had to decide that very day to hire him or he would be at their competition the following Monday. They hired him on the spot. Within 24 months he was one of their largest investment professionals in the country. He had now gone from selling himself to being chased by investment firms around the country. He was recruited away by one of the largest investment banking firms in the country to build out an institutional department over a three period. Having achieved the entire plan in a 12 month period he quit. Now in his late 20's he acquired his first company. After another two years and having brought his first company public he acquired his second company and then a third a fourth and more. During his career he has founded and or acquired numerous companies, funded hundreds more personally, sat on numerous boards, hired, trained and motivated thousands of employees on all levels. Some of his companies worked and some did not. He has made, lost and made again fortunes. During his career he has fought competitors and regulators and at times been both admired and despised. Throughout this he has had the pleasure to meet some of the strongest people in business. He is now sought after as a consultant and speaker on the subjects of entrepreneurship, innovation, employee motivation and leadership. His admirers refer to him as, "The Fixer".

He believes, "the day you stop innovating is the day you start dying."

You can connect with Dan on LinkedIn, it is the best way to get him a message and start a conversation or if you prefer www.danjshrader@gmail.com.

www.ingramcontent.com/pod-product-compliance
Lightning Source LLC
Chambersburg PA
CBHW060350190526
45169CB00002B/554